Fall Field Trips

Let's Go to the
Nature Center

by Lisa J. Amstutz

PEBBLE
a capstone imprint

Pebble Emerge is published by Pebble, an imprint of Capstone.
1710 Roe Crest Drive
North Mankato, Minnesota 56003
www.capstonepub.com

**Library of Congress Cataloging-in-Publication Data is available on the Library
of Congress website.**
ISBN 978-1-9771-2449-4 (library binding)
ISBN 978-1-9771-2492-0 (eBook PDF)

Summary: It's fall, and it's time to visit a nature center! Take a close look at nature,
learn how to take care of the environment, and have fun doing some nature
activities too. Through playful text and beautiful images, kids will experience what
it's like to visit a nature center.

Image Credits
iStockphoto: kali9, 6, KarenMassier, 10, SolStock, 9; Shutterstock: Artefficient,
(plaid) design element throughout, Charlotte Payne, 20, Dmytro Zinkevych, Cover,
Gerald A. DeBoer, 12, kali9, 19, Monkey Business Images, 14, Nella, 3, oliveromg,
5, Stacy Ellen, 17, SusImage, 7, Sveta Lagutina, 15, Timofey Zadvornov, 1, Tony
Baggett, 13, UnaDoradita, 16, venimo, design element throughout, Vitaly Ilyasov, 11

Editorial Credits
Editor: Shelly Lyons; Designer: Kayla Rossow; Media Researcher: Morgan Walters;
Production Specialist: Spencer Rosio

All internet sites appearing in back matter were available and accurate when this
book was sent to press.

Printed and bound in China
PO3322

Table of Contents

Words in **bold** are in the glossary.

A Trip to the Nature Center

Fall is here! The air is cool. Leaves turn red and gold. They drop to the ground. Then they dry up. *Crunch!* The leaves make noise beneath our feet.

It's time to visit the **nature** center!

This is a place to learn about nature.

We will hike trails. We will watch animals.

Someone will teach us about birds.

At the Nature Center

A **guide** welcomes us to the nature center. She tells us about the building, land, and animals here. We learn about the area's **ecosystem**.

Some small animals live in the main building. The staff take good care of them. It's feeding time for the turtles. A worker feeds them.

Let's take a hike! The path winds through the woods. Our guide leads the way. Trail markers show us where to go. We are careful not to harm plants or animals.

We listen to our guide. She tells us to stay on the path. That way we will not get lost. We will be safe. She says we should stay with the group.

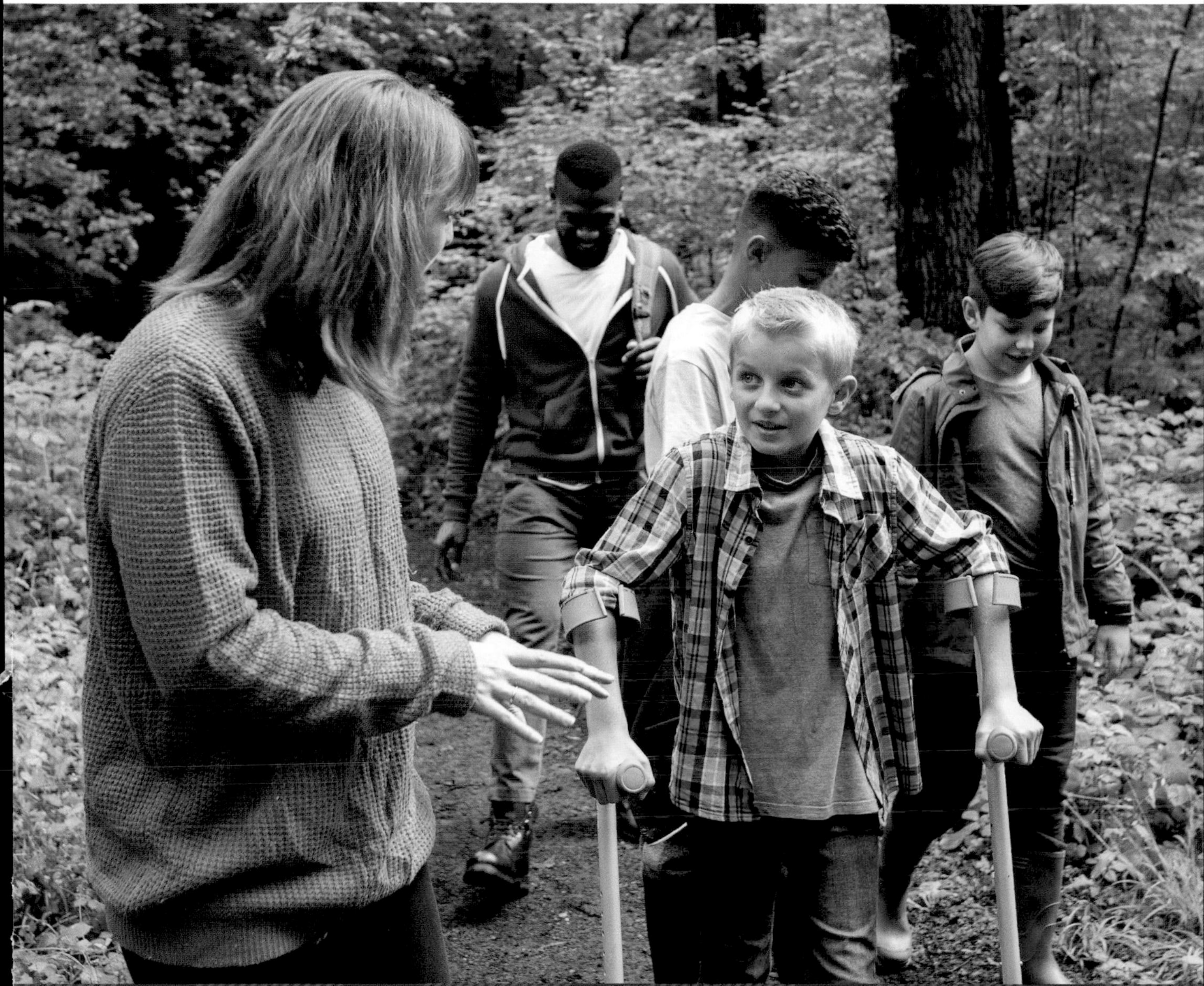

The forest is a busy place. Birds chirp in the trees. A tiny bird flies to a feeder. It picks a seed to eat. Then it returns to a branch.

A squirrel picks up nuts. A chipmunk nibbles fallen birdseed. *Hop, hop!* A toad crosses the path. A rabbit twitches its nose.

Down by the Pond

After some time, we reach the pond.
Geese honk loudly. Frogs croak. *Ribbit!*
Fish swim back and forth in the water.
We toss them food the guide gives us.

What else lives in the pond? We scoop up water with a net. We catch lots of wiggling **insects**. We even catch a snail! See its shell?

It's time for lunch! Here is a picnic table.
We sit down to eat. We eat sandwiches
and drink hot cocoa. Then we throw away
our trash.

Next, we head to the playground. Whoosh! We zoom down the slide. It's fun to climb on the wall. We crawl through tunnels and play tag.

All About Birds

Back at the main building, it's time for class. A **naturalist** teaches us about birds. We watch him band a bird's leg. The band will show **scientists** where the animal goes.

Next, we make a bird feeder. We spread peanut butter on a pine cone. Then we roll the cone in birdseed. It will feed the birds during winter.

Our class is over. It is time to leave. We say goodbye to the animals. The workers thank us for visiting. We thank them for teaching us too. Soon, we will visit the nature center again. What do you think we will see next time?

Pine Cone Bird Feeder

Make this easy feeder for birds during winter. They will love this tasty treat!

What You Need:

- yarn or string
- pine cone
- table knife
- peanut butter or sunflower butter
- birdseed
- plate

What You Do:

1. Tie the yarn or string to the top of the cone, forming a loop.

2. Use the knife to cover the pine cone with peanut butter or sunflower butter.

3. Pour birdseed onto the plate. Then roll the pine cone in the birdseed.

4. Hang your cone outdoors and watch the birds enjoy it!

Glossary

ecosystem (EE-koh-sis-tuhm)—a group of animals and plants that work together with their surroundings

guide (GIDE)—a person who leads a group

insect (IN-sekt)—a small animal with a hard outer shell, six legs, three body sections, and two antennae; most insects have wings

naturalist (NACH-ur-uh-list)—someone who studies plants, animals, and other living things

nature (NAY-chur)—everything in the world that isn't made by people

scientist (SYE-un-tist)—a person who studies the world around us